Optimizing IEEE 802.11i Resource and Security Essentials

For Mobile and Stationary Devices

Optimizing IEEE 802.11i Resource and Security Essentials

For Mobile and Stationary Devices

Parisa Naraei
Iraj Sadegh Amiri
Iman Saberi

James Yu, Technical Editor

ELSEVIER

AMSTERDAM • BOSTON • HEIDELBERG
LONDON • NEW YORK • OXFORD • PARIS
SAN DIEGO • SAN FRANCISCO
SINGAPORE • SYDNEY • TOKYO

Syngress is an Imprint of Elsevier

SYNGRESS.

Acquiring Editor: Chris Katsaropoulos
Editorial Project Manager: Benjamin Rearick
Project Manager: Preethy Simon

Syngress is an imprint of Elsevier
225 Wyman Street, Waltham, MA 02451, USA

Library of Congress Cataloging-in-Publication Data
A catalog record for this book is available from the Library of Congress

British Library Cataloguing in Publication Data
A catalogue record for this book is available from the British Library

ISBN: 978-0-12-802222-1

CONTENTS

Abstract ix

List of Tables xi

List of Figures...xiii

List of Abbreviations xv

Chapter 1   Introduction..1

1.1 Introduction 1

1.2 Problem Background...1

1.3 Problem Statement 4

1.4 Purpose of the Study..4

1.5 Objectives of the Study..5

1.6 Significance of the Study...5

1.7 Scope of the Study 5

1.8 Organization of the Study 6

1.9 Summary...6

Chapter 2   Literature Review...7

2.1 Introduction..7

2.2 Definition of Encryption in 802.11-2012......................7

2.3 History of 802.11x, Particularly 802.11-2012 7

    2.3.1 Wireless Protocol 802.11b................................10

    2.3.2 Wireless Protocol 802.11a 10

    2.3.3 Wireless Protocol 802.11g................................10

    2.3.4 Wireless Protocol 802.11n................................10

    2.3.5 Wireless Protocol 802.11-2012 11

        2.3.5.1 Wired Equivalent Privacy 11

        2.3.5.2 Wi-Fi Protected Access (WPA)............12

        2.3.5.3 Wi-Fi Protected Access 2 (WPA2) 12

        2.3.5.4 Classification of Encryption Components
             in 802.11-2012 12

2.3.6 Key Derivation Mechanism in 80211.i 13

2.3.7 Advanced Encryption Standard 13

2.3.8 CBC-MAC in 802.11-2012 15

2.3.9 AES in CTR Mode in 802.11-2012 16

    2.3.9.1 Encryption 16

    2.3.9.2 Decapsulation 17

2.4 Framework of AES-CCMP 20

2.5 Mobile Devices and Non-mobile Devices 20

2.5.1 Types of Mobile Devices 20

2.5.2 Nonmobile Devices 21

2.6 Problems of IEEE 802.11 in Nonmobile Devices
and Mobile Devices 21

2.6.1 Problems of AES-CCMP in Nonmobile Devices 21

2.6.2 Problems of AES-CCMP in Mobile Devices 23

2.7 Related Works 23

2.8 Summary 24

Chapter 3   Research Methodology 25

3.1 Introduction 25

3.2 Research Framework 25

3.3 Project Requirements 26

3.3.1 Hardware Requirements 26

3.3.2 Software Requirements 27

3.4 Data Analysis 28

3.5 Summary 28

Chapter 4   Design and Implementation for Mobile Devices 29

4.1 Introduction 29

4.2 AES-CCMP 30

4.3 AES Encryption 31

4.4 Key Expansion of AES 32

4.4.1 Counter 34

4.4.2 Convert Input Into Byte 34

4.4.3 Array Copy 35

4.4.4 Block Counter 35

4.4.5 Add Pad 35

4.4.6 Convert Data Byte to Block Byte 36

4.4.7 Encryption 37

4.4.8 Convert Block Byte Plaintext to Array Byte 38

4.4.9 Convert Byte to Output 38

4.4.10 Decryption 39

4.4.11 AES Object 39

4.5 Analysis of AES Encryption and Decryption in Rounds
     Lower Than 10 39

4.6 Analysis 40

4.6.1 Generated Key Analysis 41

4.6.2 Ciphertext Analysis Based on Incremented
       Key Values 42

4.7 Randomness of the Values 43

4.8 Attack Analysis 44

4.8.1 Brute-Force Analysis 44

4.8.2 TMTO Analysis 45

4.9 Summary 46

Chapter 5   Conclusion 47

5.1 Project Achievements 48

5.1.1 Overview of the Study 48

5.1.2 Review of the Results 48

5.1.3 Implication of the Results 49

5.1.4 Limitation of the Study 49

5.2 Recommendations 50

5.2.1 Recommendation Based on Results 50

5.2.2 Recommendation for Future Research 50

References 51

ABSTRACT

AES-CCMP128 incorporates two sophisticated cryptographic techniques that are counter mode and CBC-MAC. This is to provide a robust security protocol between the mobile clients and furthermore the mobility characteristic of mobile devices makes it difficult for an eavesdropper to spot data patterns. However, adding security functionality to mobile devices can reduce the Wi-Fi connection rate due to the limited resources of mobile devices. Therefore, the lack of balance between the security level, resource usage, and network speed required in mobile devices is eminent. The aim of this study is to speed up the Wi-Fi connection in mobile devices and also to optimize the resource usage by reducing two rounds of AES-CCMP, resulting in 20% increase in network connection speed and optimization in the resource usage of mobile devices. Round 8 and round 9 of AES-CCMP are the suggested results, named "Short Time" (ST) and "Long Time" (LT) usage of mobile devices for less than 2 h and more than 2 h, respectively. On the other hand, nonmobile devices do not have the same restrictions; instead, they have higher CPU, memory, battery charge, and hardware. But, on the other hand, the stationary characteristic makes nonmobile device an easy target to attack. Therefore, the security level they require is higher in comparison to that of mobile devices but the resource usage is yet to be optimized. Consequently, the possibility of AES-256 in nine rounds has been investigated in this study for nonmobile devices considering Moore's law and, as such, 10% optimization has been achieved in the resource usage. The proposed scenarios of ST and LT are implemented by using C# language and the results are gained from execution time, memory usage, avalanche effect, and crypt analysis for nonmobile and mobile devices.

Keywords: AES- CIA-CCMP- IEEE- Mobile Devices, Vulnerabilities, Encryption, Decryption, WEP

LIST OF TABLES

Table 2.1 802.11x Families 9

Table 2.2 WLAN Frequencies and Data Rates................................. 10

Table 4.1 Comparison Between Resources of a Sample
iPhone and MacBook Pro.. 41

Table 4.2 Percentage of Avalanche Effect in 1-Bit
Change of Generated Key 41

Table 4.3 Percentage of Avalanche Effect in the Ciphertext
Based on Incremental Key.. 42

Table 4.4 Results of Frequency Test....................................... 44

Table 4.5 Results of Runs Test 44

Table 4.6 TMTO Required Time on Rounds 5–10 46

Table 4.7 AES-CCMP Proposed Modes 46

LIST OF FIGURES

Fig. 2.1 Mapping IEEE 802.11 to OSI model. 8

Fig. 2.2 Key generation mechanism in 802.11-2012. 13

Fig. 2.3 Main construction of AES algorithm:
(left) encryption and (right) decryption. 14

Fig. 2.4 The first block format of CBC-MAC. 15

Fig. 2.5 Constructing of Nonce for CBC-MAC. 16

Fig. 2.6 CBC-MAC structures in 802.11-2012. 16

Fig. 2.7 The first block format of IC. 17

Fig. 2.8 AES-CCMP (encryption). 18

Fig. 2.9 Decryption stages and MIC authentication
in AES-CCMP. 19

Fig. 3.1 Research framework. 27

Fig. 4.1 802.11i CBC –MAC Structure for
Authentication-Integrity. 31

Fig. 4.2 IC scheme. 31

Fig. 4.3 AES-CCMP encryption process. 32

Fig. 4.4 The relation between different components of AES. 33

Fig. 4.5 Key generation. 33

Fig. 4.6 Pseudocode for key expansion. 34

Fig. 4.7 Pseudocode for convert input into byte function. 35

Fig. 4.8 Pseudocode for array copy function. 35

Fig. 4.9 Pseudocode for block counter function. 36

Fig. 4.10 Pseudocode for add pad function. 36

Fig. 4.11 Pseudocode for convert data byte to block byte
function. 37

Fig. 4.12 Pseudocode for encapsulation function. 37

Fig. 4.13 Pseudocode for convert block byte plaintext to
array byte function. 38

Fig. 4.14 Pseudocode for convert byte to output function. 38

Fig. 4.15 Pseudocode for decryption function. 39

Fig. 4.16 Data flow in encryption phase of AES-CCMP. 40

Fig. 4.17 Percentage of avalanche effect in 1-bit change
of generated key. 42

Fig. 4.18 Percentage of avalanche effect in 1-bit change of key. 43

LIST OF ABBREVIATIONS

AES	Advanced Encryption Standard
AS	authentication server
CBC	cipher block chaining
CIA	confidentiality, integrity, and availability
CTR	counter
DES	Data Encryption Standard
DLS	Direct Link Setup
GTK	Group Temporal Key
IEEE	Institute of Electrical and Electronic Engineers
ISM	industrial, scientific, and medical
IV	initial vector
KCK	Key Conformation Key
KEK	Key Encryption Key
LAN	local area network
LLC	logical link control
LT	Long Time
MAC	message authentication code
MIC	message integrity code
MIMO	Multiple-Input, Multiple-Output
MPDU	MAC Protocol Data Unit
NIST	National Institute of Standards and Technology
PHY	physical
PMK	Pairwise Master Key
PN	packet number
PTK	Pairwise Transient Key
QoS	quality of service
RADIUS	Remote Access Dial-In User Service
RF	radio frequency
RSNA	robust security network association
ST	Short Time
TK	Temporal Key
TKIP	Temporal Key Integrity Protocol

TMTO	time–memory trade-off
WEP	Wired Equivalent Privacy
WPA	Wireless Protected Access
WPA2	Wi-Fi Protected Access 2

CHAPTER 1

Introduction

1.1 INTRODUCTION

Nowadays everywhere, wireless technology can be found. Different users are using wireless technology and a wide range of wireless devices exists such as PCs, laptops, tablets, and smartphones. Wireless transmissions use the microwave technology [1–7]. The available frequencies are situated around the 2.4 GHz ISM band for a bandwidth of about 83 MHz and around the 5 GHz U-NII band, for a bandwidth of about 300 MHz divided into two parts. The accurate frequency allocations are set by laws in different countries; the same laws also adjust the maximum selected transmission power and location. Although this technology is being generally used, different devices have different capabilities in the usage. Since wireless networks have more vulnerabilities than other types of computer networks, preparing security in wireless local area network is more essential. The security mechanism chosen for different devices may differ. A satisfactory security technique in wireless network is a balance between data security and network performance. The era of wireless and wired communication systems has gained considerable attention to be a main building block of communications standards such as IEEE 802.11a/g when the microring resonators are used.

This chapter discusses the problem background of IEEE 802.11 standards and determines security model of 802.11 named 802.11-2012. Besides, it explains the aim of this research and defines objectives and the scope of this study.

1.2 PROBLEM BACKGROUND

Nowadays, the kind of devices being used for WI-FI connection is different from previous decade. People used to connect with their PCs and laptops, but nowadays they use mobile devices rather than nonmobile devices. The new mobile devices need security for the data transmission on the Internet, so the necessity of secure algorithms and protocols for encryption and decryption of the data becomes more and more important. For this purpose, new devices had to follow the existing security protocols that were designed and implemented on nonmobile devices for Wi-Fi connections.

The IEEE 802.11 standard defines an interface between a wireless client and an access point (AP) or in ad hock networks. IEEE 802.11-2012 is a revision to the original IEEE 802.11. The draft standard was sanctioned by the IEEE on June 24, 2004. This standard specifies security mechanisms for wireless networks. For confidentiality 802.11-2012 uses a new model of encryption. The new cryptography is based on the Advanced Encryption Standard (AES) algorithm, which was selected by NIST and adopted by the US government as a national standard, and replacement for the previous standard is based on the Data Encryption Standard (DES) algorithm. Strong encryption and authentication are added as the primary components of 802.11-2012 to enhance the original 802.11 standard [8].

The encryption methods of three generations of 802.11-2012 are described as follows:

Wired Equivalent Privacy (WEP): Uses the RC4 stream cipher for providing confidentiality, and the ICV (CRC-32) for integrity. Some of the weaknesses of WEP refer to not being able to stop packet forgery and replay attacks. Also attackers can easily record and replay packets. WEP uses RC4 inappropriately [9]. Keys are not strong, and attacker can do brute-force attack in less than an hour. This protocol reuses initialization vectors. Some attack techniques are able to decrypt data without key and it allows an intruder to invisibly modify a plaintext without having the key for encryption. Besides, key management is weak and upgrading is not perfect. There are some problems in the RC4 algorithm and in WEP message authentication can be easily forged. There are four scenarios for attacking WEP:
Scenario one: Pulling packets from captured data
Scenario two: Interactively pulling packets from live communication
Scenario three: Creating a packet from a chopchop replay attack
Scenario four: Creating a packet from a fragmentation attack

TKIP(): The WPA as the certification of TKIP was developed for solving the issues in the WEP method, without any changes in hardware. This standard identifies two modes, which are personal and enterprise mode. In addition, the TKIP has following weaknesses [10]:

1. Brute-force attack
2. Dictionary attack

In the context of security, a brute-force attack is a particular strategy used to break your crafted password. This is the most widely used method of cracking and dictionary attack is a technique for defeating a cipher or authentication mechanism by trying to determine its decryption key or passphrase by trying likely possibilities, such as words in a dictionary.

Wi-Fi Protected Access II (WPA2): WPA2 came after two generations of 802.11-2012, which are WEP and WPA; they used RC4-CRC and RC4-TKIP/MIC in order. WPA2 is known as the best security protocol in wireless networks. It replaces RC4 with AES and substitutes MIC with message authentication code. Same as WPA, WPA2 supports two security modes. The first mode is personal and the second mode is enterprise [10].

1. A preshared secret is used for home or personal use. Clients and APs are manually configured to use the same secret of up to 64 ASCII characters or 256 bits.
2. 802.11-2012 adopts 802.1X for user authentication in enterprise mode. 802.1X is based on EAP and defines the framework of authentication. It does not include the authentication methods, but supports multiple authentication methods, such as EAP-TLS and EAP-TTLS. EAP-TLS delivers a much stronger authentication mechanism, and secure key distribution.

Authentication is the assurance that an entity is who he/she/it claims to be. Confidentiality "implies a relationship between two or more persons in which the information communicated between them is to be kept in confidence." And integrity is the accuracy and consistency of stored data, indicated by an absence of any alteration in data between two updates of a data record. According to these definitions, 802.1X is used for authentication. Encryption (CCMP) is used for confidentiality, and MIC is for data integrity.

MAC, although called authentication, is for the "authentication" of the message, and it is better called data integrity. The authentication of the communication is via 802.1X. Internet connection speed and broadband connectivity has reached 17.5 Mbps in the world but such a net speed is not achieved in wireless networks yet. The high-capacity transmission of data can be achieved using multiple signals. The strong security protocol of AES-CCMP (WPA2) slows down the wireless speed. Despite the popularity of mobile devices, their performance and energy bottlenecks remain hidden due to a lack of visibility into the resource-constrained mobile execution environment with potentially complex interaction with the Wi-Fi connection. AES-CCMP is working tardily in mobile devices with resource limitation, and preparing ideal encryption in AES-CCMP leads to speed reduction and this is the issue that should be looked into.

1.3 PROBLEM STATEMENT

IEEE 802.11-2012 encryption technique provides strong security mechanism in computer systems but it is not optimized in the usage of resources. Besides, in mobile devices that are power- and resource-constrained, the wireless connection speed decreases. The level of security provided in AES-CCMP is more than that needed in mobile devices since the mobility characteristic of mobile devices restricts the time required by an attacker to hack the victim device and the session would be terminated whenever the location of mobile device changes. So there is a lack of balance between security level and resource usage that should be investigated.

1.4 PURPOSE OF THE STUDY

Nowadays, the number of wireless devices is growing significantly, but they all used to be computer systems. Wireless technology was not accessible in mobile and portable devices until in recent years. The purpose of this research is to determine the existing issues of the performance in current AES-CCMP encryption methods running on different types of devices and handle it so that an optimized resource usage would be achieved with the required security. Finally, two modes for 802.11-2012 for two different groups of devices will be created and evaluated with current encryption method for AES-CCMP to compare the performance.

1.5 OBJECTIVES OF THE STUDY

To achieve the intention of the study, the following objectives are specified:

1. To implement the components of AES-CCMP and to analyze the performance
2. To create two modes that are short time and long time usage for AES-CCMP, for portable systems that have resource limitation like mobile devices
3. To test and validate the possibility of optimizing resource usage in nonmobile devices

1.6 SIGNIFICANCE OF THE STUDY

Based on the issue of an increase in the number of mobile and portable devices such as tablets and smartphones that have limited resources as well as the security mechanism of AES-CCMP being run on these devices that have made them slow in term of wireless connections, offering an optimized technique for decreasing the mentioned issue will make the mobile devices faster in a Wi-Fi connection. It is able to prepare a strong security and optimized resource usage for nonmobile users in terms of wireless connection and to prepare required security and higher speed for mobile device users. Mobile device users will consider required security, high-speed data transfer, and the power limitation consequently.

1.7 SCOPE OF THE STUDY

This research focuses on secure model of 802.11 standards that is named AES-CCMP in two groups of devices. Based on the resource and power limitation the two groups are divided into mobile and nonmobile devices; this study offers an improved performance of mobile devices in terms of wireless connection using IEEE 802.11-2012 standard.

1.8 ORGANIZATION OF THE STUDY

This study is divided into six chapters. This chapter describes briefly the overview of the project and understanding of the project problem background. It also includes the project scope, purpose of this research, and objectives. Chapter 2 discusses 802.11-2012 standard, encryption components in 802.11-2012, AES-CCMP framework, and the issue of AES-CCMP in mobile devices. The methodology of this research is explained in detail in Chapter 3. Chapter 4 contains explanations of design and implementation of this study for mobile devices. Finally, Chapter 5 reviews and summarizes the whole project findings and suggests some recommendations.

1.9 SUMMARY

WLAN has a good future with 802.11 as a perfect standard to adopt in LAN environments. Also, 802.11 offers reliability and strong security. This chapter illustrates the 802.11-2012 standard. Then this chapter defines statement of the issues in performance of AES-CCMP encryption protocols in mobile devices. In addition, it explains the purpose of this research and defines objectives and scope of the study.

CHAPTER 2

Literature Review

2.1 INTRODUCTION

This chapter is about 802.11x families, particularly about 802.11-2012, and meaning of encryption in 802.11-2012; it also presents a list of encryption protocols in 802.11-2012. Besides, it explains current protocols being used for encryption of 802.11-2012 standard. Also in this chapter nonmobile and mobile devices are identified.

2.2 DEFINITION OF ENCRYPTION IN 802.11-2012

According to *Britannica Concise Dictionary* "data encryption" is the process of disguising information as "ciphertext" or data that will be unintelligible to an unauthorized person. Also, "decryption" is the process of converting ciphertext back into its original format, sometimes called plaintext. In addition, 802.11-2012 is enhanced protocol of original IEEE 802.11. This standard clearly describes security mechanisms for wireless networks.

2.3 HISTORY OF 802.11X, PARTICULARLY 802.11-2012

The IEEE 802.11 standards are set of growing specifications that are suggested by the Institute of Electrical and Electronic Engineers (IEEE). The goal of IEEE 802.11 working group was to make group of standards for WLAN process in the forbidden locations of industrial, scientific, and medical (ISM) frequency band. IEEE 802.1x authentication requires three stations in place: the supplicant that is the user or client that wants to be authenticated, the authentication server (AS), and a device that will pass information between the supplicant and the AS called the authenticator [11].

IEEE 802.11 standard covers the first and second layers of the OSI model. This standard depicts the media access control (MAC) and

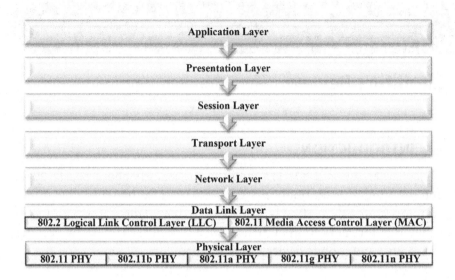

Fig. 2.1. Mapping IEEE 802.11 to OSI model.

physical layers for local area network (LAN) by wireless connectivity. 802.11 addresses LAN when the connected devices pass along other devices that are in the same area near each other. Similar to old-style wired Ethernet networks built on IEEE 802.3 standard, data link layer is divided into the logical link control (LLC) and MAC sublayers. PHY layer is responsible for radio-frequency (RF) transmission and describes frequencies and methods of modulation.

Figure 2.1 illustrates the mapping standards of IEEE802.11 to seven layers of OSI model; it is clear that 802.11 standards fall within data link and physical layers. Table 2.1 is the list of standards of 802.11 (802.11x) that were approved by IEEE WG.

The mentioned standards define the wireless connections between computers or devices of a network. Commonly, most WLANs are built on the 802.11a, 802.11b, or 802.11g standards, and recently some of them are based on 802.11ac standard. Based on the needs, selection of standards such as speed and communication ranges, level of security, noise and conflict issues, compatibility concerns, and expense happens. The following is a short explanation about the four most applicable 802.11 protocols (a, b, g, and n) and secure standard of 802.11.

Table 2.1 802.11x Families

Standard	Description	Year
802.11a	54 Mbps data rate, 5 GHz frequency band	Ratified in 1999, shipping products in 2001
802.11b	11 Mbps data rate, 2.4 GHz frequency band	1999
802.11c	Operation of bridge links	Moved to 802.1D in 2001
802.11d	Worldwide compliance with regulations for use of wireless frequency band	2001
802.11e	Supports quality of service (QoS)	2005
802.11f	Inter-Access Point Protocol recommendation for communication between access points to support roaming clients	2003
802.11g	54 Mbps data rate, 2.4 GHz frequency band	2003
802.11h	Enhanced version of 802.11a to support European controlling requirements	2003
802.11-2012	Enhanced security for the 802.11X	2004
802.11j	Enhancements to 5 GHz frequency band to support Japanese controlling requirements	2004
802.11k	Radio resource measurement enhancements	2008
802.11l	Skipped to avoid mistake with 802.11-2012	—
802.11m	Maintenance of 802.11X documentation	First draft in 2003
802.11n	>100 Mbps data rate improvements over 802.11g, higher-throughput improvements using Multiple-Input, Multiple-Output (MIMO) antennas	2009
802.11o	Skipped	—
802.11p	Wireless access for the vehicular environment	2010
802.11q	Skipped	—
802.11r	Fast roaming support by basic service set transitions	2008
802.11s	ESS mesh networking for access points	2010
802.11t	Wireless performance prediction, recommendation for testing standards	Cancelled
802.11u	Internetworking with 3G, cellular, and other forms of external networks	2010
802.11v	Wireless network management and device configuration	2010
802.11w	Enhanced security of Protected Management Frames	2009
802.11x	Skipped (generic name for the 802.11 family)	—
802.11y	Contention-based protocol for interference prevention	2008
802.11z	Extensions to Direct Link Setup (DLS)	2010

2.3.1 Wireless Protocol 802.11b

Wireless protocol 802.11b was the first 802.11 standard with salable products available. This standard called Wi-Fi covers large areas. It works in the unlicensed 2.4 GHz radio range and passes on information at speed up to 11 Mbps in 30 m range. This standard is affected by interference from any device that operates at this frequency band and Bluetooth equipment that are able to reduce speed of transfer.

2.3.2 Wireless Protocol 802.11a

Wireless protocol 802.11a is more beneficial than Wi-Fi. It works in less-known and unlicensed frequency band (5.15–5.35 GHz) and so it is less influenced by the conflict. 802.11a uses more bandwidth than 802.11b, with a theoretic highest data rate of 54 Mbps. But actual output is frequently close to 25 Mbps.

2.3.3 Wireless Protocol 802.11g

The most known format at the present time is the wireless protocol 802.11g. It mixes the speed of the IEEE 802.11a and is backward compatible with IEEE 802.11b. This standard works in the same frequency band as 802.11b, so it is affected by the same interference.

2.3.4 Wireless Protocol 802.11n

The recent standard that is implemented is the wireless protocol 802.11n. This standard was certified in September 2009. The aim of IEEE 802.11n is to significantly raise the rate of data throughput. Both 2.4 and 5 GHz frequency bands are provided by this standard.

Table 2.2 shows frequency bands and maximum data rates described by 802.11 a, b, g, and n standards, which are ordered by year of being authorized.

Table 2.2 WLAN Frequencies and Data Rates			
IEEE Standard	Year Ratified	Maximum Data Rate (Mbps)	Frequency Band (GHz)
802.11b	1999	11	2.4
802.11a	2001	54	5.0
802.11g	2003	54	2.4
802.11n	2009	600	2.4 and 5.0

2.3.5 Wireless Protocol 802.11-2012

In wireless LAN, encryption assures privacy. Encryption is an optional field in IEEE 802.11 data frame. Without encryption, other devices are able to sniff all transmission data in wireless LAN.

There are three generations of security standards described as follows:

1. Wired Equivalent Privacy (WEP)
2. TKIP – Wireless Protected Access (WPA)
3. CCMP – WPA2

2.3.5.1 Wired Equivalent Privacy

WEP uses the RC4 algorithm to encrypt the packets of information as they are sent out from the access point or wireless network card. As soon as the access point receives the packets sent by the user's network card, it decrypts them.

Each byte of data will be encrypted using a different packet key. This ensures that if a hacker does manage to crack this packet key, the only information that is leaked is that which is contained in that packet.

The actual encryption logic in RC4 is very simple. The plaintext is XOR-ed with an infinitely long keystream. The security of RC4 comes from the secrecy of the packet key that's derived from the keystream.

WEP has following weaknesses:

1. WEP cannot stop packet forgery.
2. WEP cannot stop replay attacks. Attackers can easily record and replay packets.
3. WEP uses RC4 inappropriately. IV is not encrypted at the beginning, and attacker can do brute-force attack in less than 1 min.
4. WEP reuses initialization vectors. Some attack techniques are able to decrypt data without key.
5. WEP allows an intruder to invisibly modify a plaintext without having the key for encryption.
6. WEP allows easy forging of message authentication.

2.3.5.2 Wi-Fi Protected Access (WPA)

The WPA was developed for solving the issues in the WEP method, without any changes in hardware. This standard identifies two modes, which are personal and enterprise mode, similar to WEP. In addition, the WPA has following weaknesses:

1. Brute-force attack
2. Dictionary attack

In the context of security, a brute-force attack is a particular strategy used to break your crafted password. This is the most widely used method of cracking and dictionary attack is a technique for defeating a cipher or authentication mechanism by trying to determine its decryption key or passphrase by trying likely possibilities, such as words in a dictionary.

2.3.5.3 Wi-Fi Protected Access 2 (WPA2)

A version of the original 802.11 is 802.11-2012. Draft of this standard was approved by the IEEE on June 24, 2004. The focus of this standard is on security issues for WLANs. At the present time this standard is named WPA2 and provides confidentiality and integrity using AES-CCM protocol.

WPA was provided as an impermanent solution; WPA2 is a strong method for lots of reasons. Encryption and decryption algorithm was one of the most important reasons. In October 2000, the National Institute of Standards and Technology (NIST) voted Advanced Encryption Standard (AES) as a strong substitution to the old Data Encryption and decryption Standard. WPA2 came after two generations of 802.11-2012, which are WEP and WPA; they used RC4-CRC and RC4-TKIP/MIC in order. WPA2 is known as the best security protocol in wireless networks. It exchanged RC4 with AES and substituted Michael by message authentication code. Similar to WPA, WPA2 supports two security modes. The first mode is personal and the second mode is enterprise [10].

2.3.5.4 Classification of Encryption Components in 802.11-2012

IEEE 802.11-2012 uses AES 128 in CTR mode to encrypt data and warrant confidentiality; however, CBC-MAC mode is employed to create MIC in order to warrant integrity. Similar Temporal Key (TK) is used in the two modes.

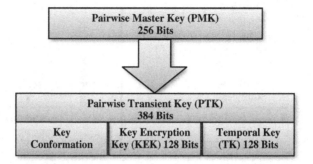

Fig. 2.2. Key generation mechanism in 802.11-2012.

2.3.6 Key Derivation Mechanism in 80211.i

The key generation technique in 802.11-2012 construction begins with authentication and authorization. 802.11-2012 protocol creates random key suitable employed with AS and petitioner to extract the Pairwise Master Key (PMK).

After that AS transfers PMK to authenticator in a secured tunnel. Remote Access Dial-In User Service (RADIUS) server is proposed as AS to use for moving PMK to authenticator. Then both authenticator and supplicant create 384-bit Pairwise Transient Key (PTK) that contains a 128-bit Key Encryption Key (KEK), a 128-bit Key Conformation Key (KCK), and a 128-bit TK [12,13].

Figure 2.2 illustrates the key generation mechanism in 802.11-2012 for creating KCK, KEK, and TK.

2.3.7 Advanced Encryption Standard

A block cipher is a deterministic and computable function of k-bit keys and n-bit (plaintext) blocks to n-bit (ciphertext) blocks. This means, when you encrypt the same plaintext block with the same key, you'll get the same result. (We normally also want that the function is invertible, i.e., given the key and the ciphertext block, we can compute the plaintext.) A stream cipher is a function that directly maps k-bit keys and arbitrary-length plaintexts to (same arbitrary-length) ciphertext, in such a way that prefixes of the plaintext map to prefixes of the ciphertext, i.e., we can compute the starting part of the ciphertext before the trailing part of the plaintext is known. (Often the message sizes might be limited to multiples of some "block size," too, but usually with smaller blocks like whole bytes or such.)

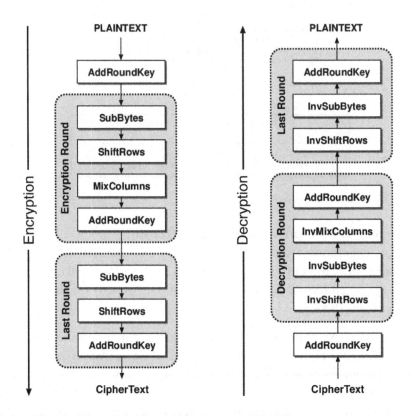

Fig. 2.3. Main construction of AES algorithm: (left) encryption and (right) decryption.

AES is a symmetric block cipher encryption that receives 128-bit size for each block and the size of key is 128, 192, and 256 bits. AES procedure involves some encryption rounds (Nr), which are determined by the cipher key size. The mentioned standard uses 10 rounds in AES-128, 12 rounds in AES-192, and 14 rounds in AES-256. Through encryption, every round is collected as a set of four main transformations. Decryption mechanism uses the inverse of mentioned procedures in reverse order. Figure 2.3 displays the main construction of the encryption and decryption in AES method. Each round covers four main transformations: Sub Byte, Shift Row, Mix Column, and Add Round Key [14].

1. SubByte: A nonlinear replacement byte that works individually on each state byte by using a table of substitution
2. ShiftRow: Cyclic shifting over different bytes offsets numbers
3. MixColumn: Column with column multiplication
4. AddRoundKey: Adding a round key to the state with a simple XOR process [14]

Figure 2.3 illustrates the main AES construction in encryption and decryption phases, which includes four basic transformations.

2.3.8 CBC–MAC in 802.11-2012

Before beginning the encryption procedure, it is necessary to organize all pieces of the MAC Protocol Data Unit (MPDU); as shown in Figure 11.16, three pieces are:

1. The MAC header (the variable parts of MAC header are masked with 0)
2. Plaintext PDU
3. The CCMP header
4. The data in plaintext form

Both MAC and CCMP headers are not encrypted; however, they have to be secured by the MIC. Mentioned parts are joined to shape authenticated data. First act after collecting mentioned parts is to compute MIC.

The MIC computation process starts by creation of packet number (PN) with joining Nonce, Flags, and payload length fields. Nonce is a distinctive field and never repetitive for similar TK. This is made with computation of CBC-MAC above the data part in packet. Most significant 8 octets (64 bits) of the output of CBC-MAC are used as MIC, which is attached to data for encrypting with CTR mode.

Calculating MIC is completed by employing CBC-MAC that encrypts a beginning block and then sequentially XORs following blocks and encrypts the result. Last MIC is 128 bits; however, only 64 bits are necessary; thus, for CCMP, the 64 lower bits of the outcome are rejected. The first block template of CBC-MAC is illustrated in Figure 2.4 including a Nonce, Flag, and D-Len.

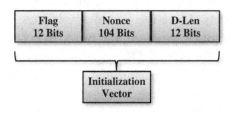

Fig. 2.4. The first block format of CBC-MAC.

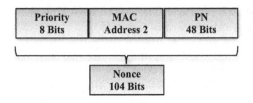

Fig. 2.5. CBC-MAC structures in 802.11-2012.

The CCMP has to save a sequence counter, named PN, that increases for every processed packet. Mentioned PN avoids intruder to reprocess a packet that has been sent before. Length of PN is 48 bits, and it is sufficiently large to ensure it never overflows.

Once first block is ready, the MIC is calculated, combining the clear text data. For the purpose of CCMP the data and the authenticated data in plaintext form must be padded to a precise block number. The MIC calculation procedure is shown in Figure 2.5.

Figure 2.5 elucidates the MIC calculation procedure in CBC-MAC structure. First of all, this procedure encrypts IV in first block and then the message is XOR-ed by the encrypted IV. After that the XOR-ed message is re-encrypted with AES. The outcome that is encrypted is used as IV in next phase in the chain of AES encryptions and XOR MIC is created.

2.3.9 AES in CTR Mode in 802.11-2012

Encryption and decryption are included in AES CTR mode. Each of them is defined isolated.

2.3.9.1 Encryption

The encryption process starts with computation of Nonce encryption in AES CTR mode and then it joins PN, Priority, and MAC Address 2 (A2) parts. This step is pursued by forming the IC with joining Nonce, Flag, and CTR parts. There are lots of similarities in the structure of Nonce in IC and Nonce structure in CBC-MAC. The IC value is used as the initial vector for AES CTR mode that runs recurrently with increasing the value of CTR in each round until finishing data included in MPDU is encrypted [15]. Figure 2.6 illustrates the first block format of IC that includes a Nonce (Priority, MAC A2, and PN), Flag, and CTR.

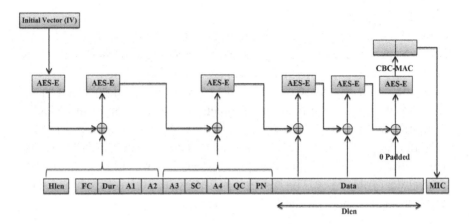

Fig. 2.6. The first block format of IC.

Following step is for data encryption of MPDU after MIC is calculated and appended to plaintext. The encryption method uses CTR mode and begins with the data immediately following the CCMP header in the pattern. Data that is encrypted is substituted with the original data for the complete data part and the MIC results in encrypted MPDU that is ready to transmit. The CTR increases only one unit for each block.

In CTR mode, the value of IC is encrypted, and then the 128-bit result is XOR-ed by the plaintext. Values of Count are modified at each block. So it must be updated in each block; however, it updates just one unit in WLAN.

CTR increasing and processing is recurrent to create the following ciphertext block. Process operates repetitively until the encrypted ciphertext is achieved. So, in CTR mode, security of the construction depends on the key that is used and the IC value [12]. Figure 2.7 shows the processes of AES-CCMP in encryption and authentication.

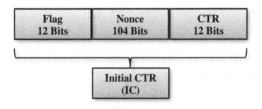

Fig. 2.7. AES-CCMP (encryption).

2.3.9.2 Decapsulation

Only AES encryption processes are needed for CCMP and not AES decryption procedures in decryption phase. Decryption uses AES CTR mode to re-create plaintext from encrypted MPDU. Then MIC is created utilizing CBC-MAC mode. For verifying which data was not altered through transition and guaranteeing integrity, computed MIC is compared with MIC attached in the MPDU. So the same input is used in both decryption and encryption stages. When an encrypted MPDU is sent to the receiver, the initial step of the receiver would be catching the correct decryption key. The right pairwise keys are then chosen based on MAC address – A2 – in the MAC header.

The receiver has to go through some steps for extracting and checking the received data validity. Decryption phase has just one stage. The PN is sent unencrypted in CCMP header. The initial action that receiver does is to read the PN and compare it with the previous received packet. In case the PN is equal to or lower than previous one, it has to be rejected as a replay of a previous message. In mentioned position receiver cannot trust the MPDU.

If the PN equals the previous one, the following stage is to set up AES CTR mode for decryption. It requires calculation of the initial value for the CTR that has to equal the value employed in encryption. Sequential CTR values are encrypted and XOR-ed by received MPDU to return unencrypted data and the MIC.

To verify the MIC, the following step has to be taken. MIC is recalculated by the receiver original MPDU. In case the data or frame header is unaltered, and correct secret key is used, the same MIC is achieved. This MIC could be matched with MIC value sent by the frame: a match has the meaning of valid frame. A mismatch is a high probable sign of an attack and frame is rejected. When the MPDU is decoded, the MIC and CCMP header are dismissed. In Figure 2.8 the decryption stages and MIC authentications in AES-CCMP are shown.

2.4 FRAMEWORK OF AES–CCMP

CCMP procedure is built on AES process in the CTR mode and (?) CCM mode of process. By combining the CTR mode privacy and

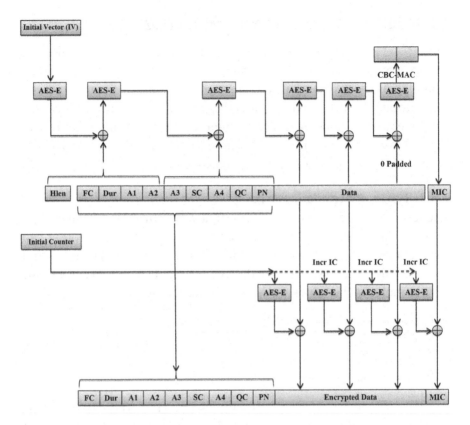

Fig. 2.8. Decryption stages and MIC authentication in AES-CCMP.

CBC-MAC authentication, the CCM works. Only 128-bit block ciphers can use CCM.

The CCM is based on block cipher mode of authentication and encryption. For general CCM mode two factors of selection (?) exist. First one is the selection of M, the length of authentication field. The selection of the M value includes a balance between the message and the probability of altering the message by an intruder. 4, 6, 8, 10, 12, 14, and 16 octets are legal values. The second one is selection of L, the length of the field size. Mentioned value needs a trade-off among the maximum size of message and Nonce size. Different uses need different trade-offs, so L is a parameter. Legal values of L range among 2 and 8 octets ($L = 1$ is reserved). M is the number of octets in authentication field 3 bits ($M - 2$)/2; L is the number of octets in length field 3 bits $L - 1$ (VOCAL, 2003).

2.5 MOBILE DEVICES AND NON-MOBILE DEVICES

Mobile devices usually are of small size and easily portable, and the battery would need to recharge frequently. A mobile device, also called a handheld device or handheld computer, is a pint-sized computing device. Mobile devices usually go together with a touch or nontouch display screen and, sometimes, even a mini keyboard. Nonmobile devices do not have power limitation. They move less frequently and have higher capabilities (?) in terms of CPU and hardware.

2.5.1 Types of Mobile Devices

The term mobile device is used to mean a wide range of consumer electronics. Usually mobile device is used to describe the devices that can connect to the Internet. However, some will classify digital cameras and standard MP3 players as mobile devices as well. The category of mobile devices includes the following devices, as well as others:

1. Personal digital assistant (PDA)
2. Smartphones
3. Tablet PC
4. Phablet (smartphones)

   PDAs and smartphones are among the most preferred mobile devices, which offer all the conveniences of a personal computer, along with a very small form factor. Examples of PDA devices are PalmPilot, Revo, Sony Clie, Hewlett-Packard Jornada, Casio Cassiopeia, Compaq iPaq, and Toshiba Pocket PC. Examples of smartphones are Sony Ericsson, Palm Treo, Blackberry, Nokia T-Mobile Sidekick, Torq, Motorola Q, E-Ten, HP iPaq, and I-mate, and examples of tablet PCs are Samsung Q1, Toshiba Portege, Fujitsu Lifebook, Motion Computing, and IBM ThinkPad.

2.5.2 Nonmobile Devices

Nonmobile devices do not have power limitation. They move less and are highly configured in terms of CPU and hardware and can be categorized as follows:

1. Personal computer (desktop)
2. Laptops
3. Wireless access points

2.6 PROBLEMS OF IEEE 802.11 IN NONMOBILE DEVICES AND MOBILE DEVICES

In this section problems of IEEE 802.11-2012 in the two mentioned systems are discussed.

2.6.1 Problems of AES-CCMP in Nonmobile Devices

The AES-CCMP security construction is relying on TK used and IC. By joining Nonce, Flags, and CTR, IC is made; also Nonce is achieved by combining PN, A2, and Priority.

The prediction process of IC begins with reconstructing Nonce. Nonce is achieved by simply unifying the two fields from MAC header, called the Priority and A2, and one field from the CCMP header, named PN. 8 Priority bits are recently set to zero by default, which is kept for future usage in frame ordering. A2 is simply available with packet sniffing, employing common tools such as Wireshark (one word). So the PN field changes dynamically, and it is set to 1 each time a TK is recalculated. Therefore, rebuilding of Nonce becomes a fairly simple task.

Rebuilding Nonce is followed by computation of the IC that requires discovering values of Flags and CTR. Flag's field includes a static value that is popular (01011001). So, only CTR value is unavoidable for IC prediction procedure. The CTR value starts from 1 and increases for each block. Also the first block of each message is known, so the probability of guessing CTR value in first block is 1. In summer, without a legal procedure, IC prediction can be done easily [16].

IEEE 802.11-2012 recognizes the maximum size of MPDU as 2312 octets that includes 2296 octets data, 8 octets MIC, and 8 octets CCMP header. Therefore, Payload size converts to 2296 octets. Knowing mentioned information in CBC-MAC, bit string illustration of size of Payload field is calculated. So, without completing a legal authentication procedure, initial vector prediction can be done easily [12].

The Nonce structure technique of AES-CCMP construction in nonmobile devices being used in IEEE 802.11-2012 is weak [12]. IC prediction and TMTO attack are the most common weaknesses. "time–memory trade-off" is the generic terminology for an algorithm that improves (shortens) running time by using more space (memory), or, similarly, that improves memory usage (i.e., using less RAM or disk, or using it "better," e.g., with sequential access instead of random access) at the expense of more computing time. A much more strong solution for mentioned issues is believed to be random Nonce. Nonce randomization would increase unpredictability of the IC and conveys effective protection against the vulnerability.

By randomizing Nonce structure and increasing key length from 128 to 256 bits, all the possible attacks on confidentiality can completely be eliminated such as precomputational attack [17].

Also, AES-CCMP 256 algorithm provides optimized usage of resources and good speed such as AES-128 and high security from AES-256 [16].

In the AES-CCMP 256 encryption method, AES-256 is used instead of AES-128 and AES-CCMP 256 has solved the problems of security in classic AES-CCMP completely and also can mitigate TMTO and brute-force attacks. But AES-CCMP 256 does not solve resource usage in classic AES-CCMP while the resource usage can be reduced because in encryption phase of AES-CCMP, the goal of using AES is creating unpredictable structure to XOR with plaintext.

2.6.2 Problems of AES-CCMP in Mobile Devices

Nonmobile devices have no resource limitation and they are not easily portable, so an attacker can have the session connection during some hours, with not even the victim being aware of the attack. On the other hand, an attacker cannot keep the session connection with the mobile devices for a long time because of their mobility and it leads to the termination of the session and the attacker do not have much time to hack the victim device. The only way of keeping the session would be physically following the victim, which in most cases is impossible. So the strong security mechanism of AES-CCMP in case of mobile devices is not an optimized method when such a level of security is not needed and also it makes mobile devices face power reduction and battery charging frequently. Besides, the speed of data transfers in wireless connection decreases significantly.

2.7 RELATED WORKS

AES-CCMP is a fresh WLAN security standard that offers the maximum security level with using the most robust 128-bit AES encryption procedure for encrypting and authenticating data at the same time. The length of key employed in all modes of AES is 128 bits. Same as each modern cipher, AES-CCMP security is dependent on the key, and in this protocol also dependent on the IC value. AES CTR mode uses TK with 128-bit size, for encrypting an IC. Result is XOR-ed by the plaintext to create initial block of ciphertext.

The main sources of energy consumption during a secure wireless transaction are cryptographic computations used to establish secure sessions and for encryption and authentication and cryptographic computations used for performing secure data transactions [18].

The Nonce structure of AES-CCMP employed in IEEE 802.11-2012 is weak. The most common weaknesses are IC prediction and TMTO attack. In the latest related works execution time has increased significantly and a good cryptanalysis is not done on the presented methods. The best approach to develop Nonce structure in this procedure to avoid possibility of IC prediction is to generate random Nonce.

AES-CCMP 256 was proposed and it could provide a strong security mechanism and could mitigate some attacks being run on AES-CCMP but it is not optimized in terms of resource usage. Since mobile devices are almost new generation of technology that can connect to the Internet and have data transfer in Wi-Fi, they have to follow the classic security mechanism of AES-CCMP, which leads to speed reduction in Wi-Fi connections and makes them need battery charging.

2.8 SUMMARY

The 802.11-2012 standard served a kind of network association called robust security network association (RSNA). RSNA construction uses AES in CTR mode by CBC MAC protocol. The AESCTR mode is employed for data encryption to prepare confidentiality. When CBC mode is used, MIC is created to support data integrity and authentication of the message.

In this chapter, definition of encryption in 802.11-2012, framework of CCMP, issues of mentioned protocol in computer and mobile devices, and introduction of classification of encryption components used in 802.11-2012 were explained.

CHAPTER *3*

Research Methodology

3.1 INTRODUCTION

So far, in Chapter 2 it has been discussed that the AES-CCMP 256 construction used in 802.11-2012 standard is strong enough in nonmobile devices in terms of security but is not optimized in resource usage and also AES-CCMP that is used in mobile devices has many problems. Providing security services increases the computation and hence energy consumption due to cryptographic algorithms [19]. The main purpose of the study is to find out the issues of the current encryption methods in 802.11-2012 when used in mobile devices and propose a method for increasing the speed of wireless connection in mobile devices by creating two modes of AES-CCMP. The first mode is used in mobile devices, which provides required security and increases the wireless connection speed. The other mode provides optimized resource usage for nonmobile devices.

This chapter discusses the methodology of the study, explaining how to achieve the research objectives that are mentioned in Chapter 1. There is a list of activities needed to be followed, and they are divided into three phases. Besides, the hardware and software specifications that are used in this study are mentioned in this chapter.

3.2 RESEARCH FRAMEWORK

Research framework starts with the first phase in which classic AES-CCMP is implemented and coded. The implementation would be in counter mode. It does not use the AES block cipher directly to encrypt the data. Instead, it encrypts the value of an arbitrary value called the counter and then XORs the result with the data to produce ciphertext. Every component of AES-CCMP is analyzed and considered in implementation. The AES-CCMP security construction is relying on TK used and IC.

Next phase would be creating new modes of AES-CCMP for mobile devices. For this purpose the two optimized rounds of AES-128 are found in which the resource usage is optimized and security is provided. A proposed method in this section is analyzing different rounds of AES-CCMP before reaching the 10th round and finding the optimized round in which security is provided. Since the round is before 10, there would be a great reduction in resource usage. Following the discussed phases, the output will be new modes named AES-MD (mobile devices). Using these modes will lead to higher-speed Wi-Fi connection in mobile devices. Evaluating and testing will be done in this phase and the feedback is sent to the first phase.

The final phase would be creating optimized AES-CCMP 256 in nonmobile devices. AES-CCMP 256 construction used in 802.11-2012 standard is strong enough in nonmobile devices in terms of security but is not optimized in resource usage. For this purpose AES-CCMP 256 is created by using AES-256 in the 10th round and then AES-CCMP 256 is optimized in resource usage in nonmobile devices named AES-CCMP MC as the output of this phase. So far, it has been proved that in round 10, the strong security required can be achieved for nonmobile devices and for optimization of resource usage. It will be checked whether AES-CCMP 256 is cost-effective to run in lower rounds. Figure 3.1 shows the research framework.

3.3 PROJECT REQUIREMENTS

This section lists the software and hardware requirements that are used in this research. Especially these hardware requirements must be prepared for the proposed system to execute smoothly. The hardware and software requirements are mentioned in the following.

3.3.1 Hardware Requirements
1. Processor: Intel® Core™2 Duo T6600 @ 2.67 GHz
2. RAM: 4.00 GB
3. System type: 64-bit operating system
4. Computer type: laptop

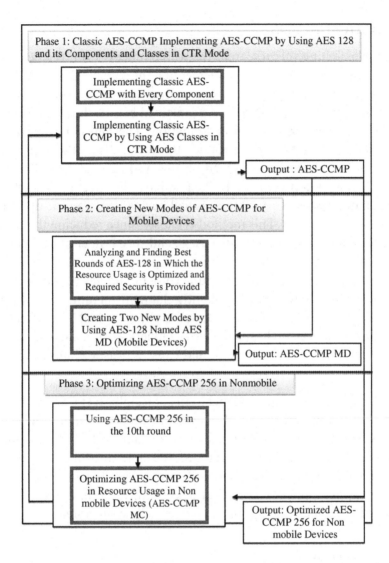

Fig. 3.1.   Research framework.

3.3.2 Software Requirements

1. Operating system: Windows 7 Professional Service Pack 1
2. Microsoft .Net Framework Version 4.0
3. Microsoft Visual Studio .Net 2012
4. Microsoft Excel 2010

3.4 DATA ANALYSIS

For implementing this research, the whole process from the beginning is implemented in C#. After implementing the classic AES-CCMP, two new modes will be suggested in this study that work for mobile devices based on experimental analysis. As explained before, the mobile devices have CPU, memory, and power limitation. The aim is to choose two modes of AES-CCMP before round 10, which satisfies the required security for mobile devices to speed up the Wi-Fi connection. The work can be divided into two parts. In the first part, the effect of 1-bit change of generated key in every 10 rounds will be analyzed and the optimized modes will be chosen. This method is chosen since reducing the rounds leads to optimization of resource usage and speed. In cryptography, the avalanche effect refers to a desirable property of cryptographic algorithms, typically block ciphers and cryptographic hash functions. The avalanche effect is evident if on slightly changing an input (e.g., flipping a single bit), the output changes significantly (e.g., half the output bits flip). In the case of high-quality block ciphers, such a small change in either the key or the plaintext should cause a drastic change in the ciphertext.

In the second part, the avalanche effect on ciphertext using incremental key values will be analyzed in every 10 rounds to figure out which rounds have the lowest possibility of predictability. It has been proven that when half of the bits are changed, the ciphertext has the least predictability. So, after the required modes are chosen based on mathematics, the required time for TMTO attacks on these optimized modes will be tested and finally the optimized modes will be suggested.

3.5 SUMMARY

In this chapter, the research methodology has been discussed and clarified, along with the software and hardware instruments that are used in this research. Research framework with three phases is illustrated to achieve research objectives that are mentioned in Chapter 1.

CHAPTER 4

Design and Implementation for Mobile Devices

4.1 INTRODUCTION

Mobile devices are power- and resource-constrained and the wireless connection speed has not reached the required speed yet. Mobile devices have hardware constraints and they are designed so that they cannot support stronger hardware. They cannot upgrade their hardware, so the best cryptographic algorithm should be chosen for them that can work in most limited hardware, while the same is not the case for nonmobile devices.

As mentioned in Chapter 1, because AES-CCMP 128 is a strong cryptographic algorithm, it makes the mobile devices slow in Wi-Fi connection, as the resources of a mobile device are limited. Considering the fact that the mobility characteristic of mobile devices restricts an attacker's required time to hack the victim device and the session would be terminated whenever the location of mobile device changes. So there is a lack of balance between security level and resource usage that this study is aimed to investigate.

CCM Mode Protocol is an encryption protocol designed for wireless LAN products running in mobile devices as well as nonmobile devices that implements the standards of the IEEE 802.11-2012 amendment to the original IEEE 802.11 standard. CCMP is an enhanced data cryptographic encapsulation mechanism designed for data confidentiality and based on the counter mode with CBC-MAC (CCM) of the AES standard. The confidentiality part of confidentiality, integrity, and authentication is provided by AES encryption; the integrity and authentication are provided by MAC. In this chapter, AES algorithm is only used to generate 128 random bits so that every block is different in 64 bits of 1's and 0's with the next block. The encryption and decryption parts of AES are not used in the implementation part and they are out of the focus of this study. For message integrity part also CBC-MAC of AES is used since it is more complex in comparison with hash function and also AES evaluates message integrity in parallel with encryption and that's the advantage of using CBC-MAC rather than hash function since in hash function first encryption is done and then hashing occurs.

There are three differences in AES-ECB and AES-CCMP algorithm. In AES-CCMP the XOR process does the encryption part but in AES-ECB the encryption is done by sub byte, shift row, mix Column, and add round key processes. Also in AES-ECB the input is the plaintext and the output is the ciphertext but in AES-CCMP there are two inputs: initial counter and the plaintext. Besides in AES-ECB there is a decryption component while there is no decryption component in AES-CCMP. Besides, in this chapter, the classic AES-CCMP is defined and the components in implementation are identified. Every component function is described in detail in Chapter 2. Also, two optimized modes named Long Time (LT) and Short Time (ST) of AES-CCMP are suggested after analyzing all rounds of AES-CCMP. LT is suggested for longer Wi-Fi connection (more than 2 h) and ST is suggested for shorter Wi-Fi connection (less than 2 h) in order to solve the mentioned problems in Chapter 2.

4.2 AES-CCMP

CCMP uses CCM that combines CTR for data confidentiality and CBC-MAC for authentication and integrity. CCM protects the integrity of both the MPDU data field and selected portions of the IEEE 802.11 MPDU header. CCMP is based on AES processing and uses a 128-bit key and a 128-bit block size. It uses CCM with the following two parameters:

- $M = 8$, indicating that the MIC is 8 octets (8 bytes)
- $L = 2$, indicating that the length field is 2 octets

Figure 2.5 illustrates the MIC calculation procedure in CBC-MAC structure. This procedure at first encrypts IV in the first block and after that message is XOR-ed by the encrypted IV. Then the XOR-ed message is encrypted with AES again. Encrypted outcome is employed as IV in following phase. In chaining of AES encryption and XOR MIC is created.

4.3 AES ENCRYPTION

Encryption in AES CTR mode starts with the computation of Nonce explained in detail in Chapter 2. This step is followed by creation of IC with joining Nonce, Flag, and CTR part. The structure of Nonce in IC is similar to Nonce structure in CBC-MAC. The IC value is used as the initial vector for AES CTR mode that runs repetitively with increasing the value of CTR in every round until finishing data included in MPDU is encrypted. The IC value as shown in Figure 4.1 is 128 bits, used as the initial vector for AES CTR mode that runs recurrently with increasing the value of CTR in each round until finishing data included in MPDU is encrypted. Also block format of IC that includes Flag, Nonce, and CTR is described in detail in Chapter 2.

Once MIC is calculated and attached to plaintext, the next step is data encryption of MPDU. The encryption method uses CTR mode and begins by the data instantly following the CCMP header in the pattern. Data that is encrypted substitutes the original data for the complete data part and the MIC, resulting in encrypted MPDU prepared to transmit. The CTR is increased only one unit for each block.

In CTR mode, value of IC has been encrypted; then the 128-bit result is XOR-ed with the plaintext. Values of counter are increased one unit in every block.

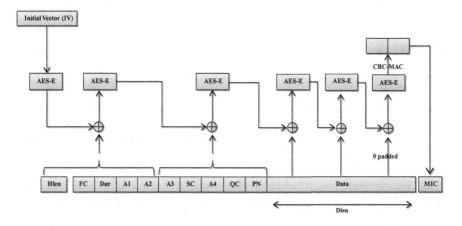

Fig. 4.1. IC scheme.

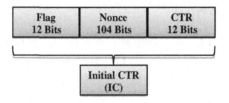

Fig. 4.2. AES-CCMP encryption process.

CTR is increased and process is repetitive to create the following ciphertext block. Process operates repetitively till encryption of ciphertext is finished. Therefore, in CTR mode, security of the construction is dependent on key that is used and the IC value. The focus of this study is on the encryption part that provides the confidentiality. Figure 4.2 shows the processes of AES-CCMP encryption.

Different components of AES-CCMP are related to either data preparation or counter preparation. Figure 4.3 shows this relation.

4.4 KEY EXPANSION OF AES

User enters the cipher key that can be very simple and easy to guess and also less than 128 bits. The key expansion of AES receives the entered key as the input and if it is less than 128 bits, it adds pad at the end of the key to make it 128 bits and performs a key expansion routine to

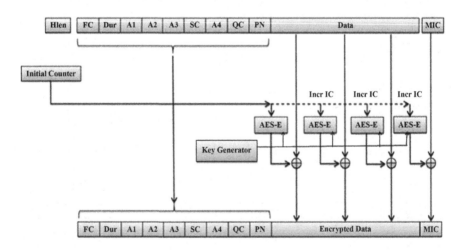

Fig. 4.3. The relation between different components of AES.

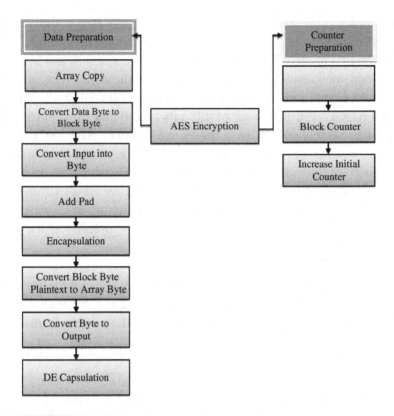

Fig. 4.4. Key generation.

generate a key schedule (Figure 4.4). The key expansion generates a total of $Nb(Nr + 1)$ words: the algorithm requires an initial set of Nb words, and each of the Nr rounds requires Nb words of key data. The resulting key schedule consists of a linear array of 4-byte words, denoted $[wi]$, with i in the range $0 < i < Nb(Nr + 1)$. Figure 4.5 contains the pseudo-code for key expansion.

As long as the key bit increases, the number of rounds the key expansion requires increases. For AES 128, the key expansion requires 10 rounds. In AES 256, the algorithms divides the 256 bits into 2 blocks of 128 bits and 14 rounds would be required for key expansion in the 2 blocks. Each

Fig. 4.5. Pseudocode for key expansion.

block consists of 128 bits, round 7 times in this case. Hence, the complexity of the key has become less. For example, if the key being entered is all 0's, in the first round of AES 128, every key bit remains 0's and in the second round, all 0's will completely change but in the same example in AES 256, in the first round, the first block of 128 bits are all 0's and also in the second round the other block of 128 bits goes 0 and from third round, they start to change. It means in the second round of AES 256, the key is still very weak and easy to guess. The longer the key length, the less is the complexity of the output key of key expansion in each round. Increasing the key length reduces the possibility of brute-force attack (from 128 to 192 bits, e.g.) and adding 2 rounds to the algorithm when changing from 128 to 192 bits is for compensating the reduced complexity of the key.

4.4.1 Counter

The counter as shown in Figure 4.1 increases only one unit for each block depending on the size of MPDU, and an increase in CTR leads to an increase of IC. The 2 bytes of hex in CTR can get the number from 0 to 2^{16}.

4.4.2 Convert Input Into Byte

Whatever data file the user wants to encrypt, whether it's a string, image, audio, or video, it should be converted into byte, because AES accepts only byte. So a convert input into byte function is required (Figure 4.6).

```
KeyExpansion(byte
key[4*Nk], word
w[Nb*(Nr+1)], Nk)
begin word temp

  i = 0

  while (i < Nk) w[i] = word(key[4*i], key[4*i+1], key[4*i+2],
      key[4*i+3]) i = i+1
  end while

  i = Nk

  while (i < Nb * (Nr+1)] temp = w[i -1] if (i mod Nk = 0)
          temp = SubWord(RotWord(temp)) xor
      Rcon[i/Nk] else if (Nk > 6 and i mod Nk = 4)
          temp = SubWord(temp) end if w[i] = w[i-Nk] xor tempi = i
      + 1
  end while end
```

Fig. 4.6. Pseudocode for convert input into byte function.

```
Function Name: Convert into Byte

byte[] convert In to Byte (Input) ;
{
byte[]IntoByte= new byte[2304];
IntoByte = GetBytes(Input);
return IntoByte;}
```

Fig. 4.7. Pseudocode for array copy function.

4.4.3 Array Copy
After the counter is increased one unit, array copy replaces the increased counter with the previous counter in initial counter and as a result the initial counter increases for one unit (Figure 4.7).

4.4.4 Block Counter
The block counter receives the 128-bit blocks and counts how many 128-bit blocks are available. In case any block is less than 128 bits, the add pad function will be called (Figure 4.8).

```
Function Name: Array copy

read ctrl[], ic[], sindex, dindex,
total, count
count = 0
while count < total
        ic [dindex] = ctrl[sindex]
        Inc count
        Inc sindex
        Inc dindex
endwhile

return new ic ;}
```

Fig. 4.8. Pseudocode for block counter function.

```
Function Name: Block Counter

Read ic
If ic%128 < > 0 then
        Increase ic.length to 128
Return new ic
```

Fig. 4.9. Pseudocode for add pad function.

4.4.5 Add Pad

The add pad function operates when the number of bits in a block is less than 128 or is not a multiplication of 128. It adds pad at the end to make the number of bits equal to 128 or a multiplication of 128 (Figure 4.9).

4.4.6 Convert Data Byte to Block Byte

This function defines a two-dimensional array in which the rows are 128 bits and the columns are the same number as "block counter" output number (Figure 4.10).

```
Function Name: Add Pad

read mpdu, mpdubypad, pad, count
mpdubypad = mpdu
if length(mpdu) % 8 <> 0 then
        pad = ((length(mpdu) / 8) + 1) * 8
        count = 0
        while count < pad
        Inc count
        mpdubypad = mpdubypad + " "
        endwhile
endif
return 128 bits MPDU block
```

Fig. 4.10. Pseudocode for convert data byte to block byte function.

```
Function Name: Convert Data Byte to Block Byte

read matris[][],pmpdu[], numberrow, i, j, k
numberrow = length(empdu) / 16
k = 0
i = 0
j = 0
while i < numberrow
        while j < 16
                matris[i,j]= pmpdu[k]
                Inc j
                Inc k
        endwhile
        Inc i
endwhile
return matrix
```

Fig. 4.11. Pseudocode for encapsulation function.

4.4.7 Encryption
Block byte is a two-dimensional array with the size of (16, data length/16). It is needed to XOR each row in the corresponding 128-bit ciphertext separately (Figure 4.11).

4.4.8 Convert Block Byte Plaintext to Array Byte
The data should be in a form of one-dimensional array for the receiver part to be acceptable (Figure 4.12).

4.4.9 Convert Byte to Output
The receiver is supposed to see the audio, video, string, or whatever he or she is expecting to see, so the output cannot be shown as byte. Therefore, a convert byte to output function is needed (Figure 4.13).

4.4.10 Decryption
The decryption process is same as encapsulation with only one difference – it XORs the data with ciphertext block byte instead of plaintext block bytes (Figure 4.14).

Function Encapsulation

read row, arrempdu [][],ciphertext[],arrpmpdu[][], tmp1,
tmp2, column

tmp1 = convert ciphertext[row] to int

tmp2 = convert arrpmpdu [row, column] to int

arrempdu[row, column] = tmp1 xor tmp2

convert arrempdu [row, column] to int

return encapsulated data

Fig. 4.12. Pseudocode for convert block byte plaintext to array byte function.

Function Name: Convert Block Byte Plaintext to Array Byte

read empdu[][], array[], numberrow, i, j, k

numberrow = length(empdu) / 16

  k = 0

  i = 0

  j = 0

while i < numberrow

  Inc j

  Inc k

endwhile

  Inc to i

Return array

Fig. 4.13. Pseudocode for convert byte to output function.

Function Name: Convert Byte to Output

Read Encapsulations data

Add header file to encapsulation data

Return encapsulation data in main format

Fig. 4.14. Pseudocode for decryption function.

```
                Function Name: Decryption

read row,  arrdmpdu [][],ciphertext[],arrempdu[][],
tmp1, tmp2, column
tmp1 = convert ciphertext[row] to int
tmp2 = convert arrempdu [row, column] to int
arrdmpdu[row, column] = tmp1 xor tmp2
convert arrdmpdu [row, column] to int


return plaintext data
```

Fig. 4.15. Data flow in encryption phase of AES-CCMP.

4.4.11 AES Object

In this part an object from the class of AES with the defined key size of 128 is identified that inherits its properties from AES. Later this object named b is ciphered with the key and the results will be given to the ciphertext. The ciphertext is empty at the beginning (Figure 4.15).

4.5 ANALYSIS OF AES ENCRYPTION AND DECRYPTION IN ROUNDS LOWER THAN 10

Round 10 has the optimized avalanche effect for diffusion and confusion and that is why it has been chosen as the number of rounds for AES 128 to run through. From round 11 and above it has fixed values. It has been tested that from round 2 and above, since rounds are corresponding, encryption and decryption can be done. The only difference is in the first and last rounds, but since they keep rounding they keep replacing and corresponding blocks neutralize each other. In AES-CCMP there is no encryption and decryption phase since encryption is done through an XOR process and XOR is reversible so it gives the initial state. It is obviously possible to work in other rounds as well. AES-128 has been broken in the seventh round. In order to break seven-round AES-128, about 2^{80} chosen plaintexts are needed; besides, the time and memory complexities are 2^{127}; thus, seven-round encryptions and 2^{65} blocks of memory of 128 bits, respectively, are required.

4.6 ANALYSIS

The new method suggested in this study is going to work for mobile devices. As explained before, the mobile devices have CPU, memory, and power limitation. The aim is to choose a mode of AES-CCMP before round 10, which satisfies the required security for mobile devices to speed up the Wi-Fi connection. The work can be divided into two parts. In the first part, the effect of 1-bit change of IC in every 10 rounds will be analyzed and the optimized modes will be chosen. This method is chosen since reducing the rounds leads to optimization of resource usage and speed. In the second part, blocks having incremental IC values and different keys will be analyzed in every 10 rounds to figure out which rounds have the lowest possibility of predictability. It has been proven that when half of the bits are changed, the ciphertext has the least predictability.

So, after the required modes are chosen based on mathematics and modeling, the required time for time–memory trade-off (TMTO) attacks on these optimized modes will be tested and finally the optimized modes will be suggested.

As shown in Table 4.1, the CPU, RAM, and power of a sample laptop is almost twice more than a mobile and since laptops have greater resources, they are able to run AES-CCMP round 10, in higher speed in comparison to mobile devices. They are stationary, so it is easier for a hacker to maintain the session connection with these devices. It can be concluded that mobile devices weaker in resources and having mobility are not as easy as laptops to be hacked and the security they need is not the same as that required by stationary devices.

4.6.1 Generated Key Analysis

The key length used in CCMP is 128 bits. Users usually tend to enter easy keys that surely are not 128 bits. So, a key generator can be used to

Table 4.1 Comparison Between Resources of a Sample iPhone and MacBook Pro			
Apple Brand	CPU (GHZ)	RAM (GB)	Power
Mobile (iPhone 5)	1.3	1	Talk time: up to 5 h on Standby time: up to 10 days
Laptop (MacBook Pro)	2.3	2.6	Up to 10 h wireless web Up to 30 days standby time

Table 4.2 Percentage of Avalanche Effect in 1-Bit Change of Generated Key									
3.06	12.77	50	49.93	50.42	50.27	49.92	50.73	49.75	49.43

create 128 bits based on what user has entered. Another method can be adding pads at the end of the key being entered, to make it 128 bits. In this section, the generated key for each 10 rounds of AES-CCMP will be changed 1 bit after the encryption to see the avalanche effect on the outputs of AES-CCMP. The results will be compared with each other and this method will be done on 500 keys that are different in 1-bit value. Then the different bits will be counted. This method is applicable from round 1 to round 10. The average of the results for every 10 rounds in 500 samples of 1-bit change in the key in the output of every two neighbor blocks is available in Table 4.2.

From the graphs in Figure 4.16, it can be inferred that, from round 3 and above the required modes have emerged. The required modes are those in which 50% have differed. Those rounds below round 3 are not suitable for our target in AES-CCMP since a hacker can easily capture some ciphertexts in these rounds and understand the pattern and in a short time he or she can obtain the key and the plaintext. For the rounds below round 3, the TMTO analysis is not needed.

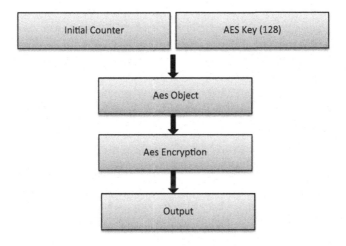

Fig. 4.16. Percentage of avalanche effect in 1-bit change of generated key.

Table 4.3 Percentage of Avalanche Effect in the Ciphertext Based on Incremental Key									
Round 1	Round 2	Round 3	Round 4	Round 5	Round 6	Round 7	Round 8	Round 9	Round 10
22.64	36.09	49.93	49.74	50.33	50.99	50.05	49.95	50.27	49.76

4.6.2 Ciphertext Analysis Based on Incremented Key Values

In this part data that is big enough to be divided into several blocks is considered. The data is 64 A's together that is being divided into 4 blocks. Each block will be encrypted with different keys, but the keys are generated by incremental values. The values of the ciphertext of each block will be compared with each other (Table 4.3).

From Figure 4.17 it can be inferred that from round 3 and above the graph shapes a line. Those are the rounds that define 50% bit difference in the ciphertext output of neighbor blocks. Considering both analyses two rounds will be omitted.

4.7 RANDOMNESS OF THE VALUES

The NIST Test Suite is a statistical package consisting of 15 tests that were developed to test the randomness of sequences produced by either

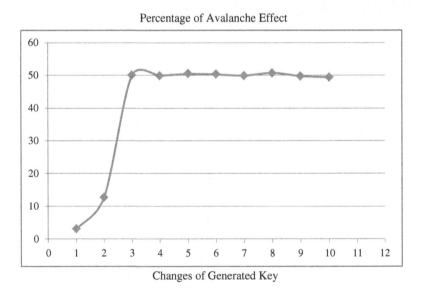

Fig. 4.17. Percentage of avalanche effect in 1-bit change of key.

Table 4.4 Results of Frequency Test

Rounds	P-Value	Result
Round 5	0.751829634045849	SUCCESS
Round 6	1	SUCCESS
Round 7	0.599426279295864	SUCCESS
Round 8	0.552919624971049	SUCCESS
Round 9	0.428291855444894	SUCCESS
Round 10	0.414216178242525	SUCCESS

hardware- or software-based cryptographic random or pseudorandom number generators. These tests focus on a variety of different types of nonrandomness that could exist in a sequence. Two of these tests – the frequency test and the runs test – are applicable for this study.

The gained values have been tested with frequency (monobit) test for each round from round 5 to 10. The n value that is the length of the bit string in this test is set to 64,000 (500 values × 128). The purpose of this test is to determine whether the number of 1's and 0's in a sequence are approximately the same as would be expected for a truly random sequence. The test assesses the closeness of the fraction of 1's to half of the values. If the P-value is ≥ 0.01, where P stands for possibility, then it's random; otherwise it is not random. Table 4.4 contains these results.

Also the randomness has been checked with runs test. The focus of this test is on the total number of runs in the sequence, where a run is an uninterrupted sequence of identical bits. A run of length k consists of exactly k identical bits and is bounded before and after with a bit of the opposite value. The purpose of the runs test is to determine whether the number of runs of 1's and 0's of various lengths is as expected for a random sequence. In particular, this test determines whether the oscillation between such 0's and 1's is too fast or too slow. The results of runs test are shown in Table 4.5.

4.8 ATTACK ANALYSIS

Brute force and TMTO are two possible attacks that should be investigated.

Table 4.5 Results of Runs Test

Rounds	P-Value	Result
Round 5	0.68950430471634	SUCCESS
Round 6	0.639039918371475	SUCCESS
Round 7	0.252409795948376	SUCCESS
Round 8	0.0434546538662177	SUCCESS
Round 9	0.571890263258181	SUCCESS
Round 10	0.963969343054186	SUCCESS

4.8.1 Brute-Force Analysis

Because of using AES, the key length in AES-CCMP is 128 bits. So, the AES-CCMP can stand against the possibility of brute force since an attacker must test 2^{128} different keys; the time taken for this is about 584,942,417,355 years (for a device that checks 2^{64} permutations per second). So 128-bit key can be used to encrypt all the packets of one message standing against the brute-force attack and that is why the key length used in this study is 128 and is not changed and all focus is on number of rounds.

4.8.2 TMTO Analysis

In this attack, attacker tries to make a balance between time and memory usage. In general, two solutions for finding n-bit key are existent:

1. Exhaustive key search: In this method, the usage of memory is zero. But the role of time is significant, and the attack should be done 2^{n-1} times (time = 2^{n-1}, memory = 0). An example of such an attack is brute-force attack.
2. Precomputation: In this method, if $C = E(P, K)$, then 2^n possible keys are created. So, the memory usage is maximum value and it is equal to 2^n. But the time needed for attack is decreased to 1 (memory = $2^n \cdot$ time = 1).

TMTO attack lies between the first and second modes and TMTO approximately requires $T = t^2$ times ($N^{1/3}$ operations per each table), $M = mt$ words of memory ($N^{1/3}$ tables, each table with $m = N^{1/3}$ words). Also, the value of N is equal to MT^2 [$N = 2^n$ (possible solutions of key)]. Letting $m = t = N^{1/3}$ results in $M = T = N^{2/3}$. So, the effective length of

Table 4.6 TMTO Required Time on Rounds 5–10

Round	TMTO (s)	TMTO/IPS
Round 5	2^{-21}	0
Round 6	1	0
Round 7	2,581,896.969	0
Round 8	6.66×10^{12}	1 h and 42 min
Round 9	1.84×10^{12}	447 years and 10 months
Round 10	2^{85}	938,609,842 years and 8 months

n-bit key is reduced to 1/3, which is equal to $2n/3$. Below is the formula of TMTO based on rounds. Table 4.6 shows the required time of TMTO attack on remaining rounds.

1. AES 128 uses 10 rounds, AES 192 uses 12 rounds, and AES 256 uses 14 rounds.
2. Equation: $R = 6 + [(\text{key length}(n)/64) \times 2]$, where R is the number of rounds.
3. Equation: $TMTO = 2^{(2/3)\times n}$, where n is the key length.
4. $TMTO = 2^{2/3(64 \times (R-6)/2)}$, replacing n with R.

The instruction per second in iPhone 5 is 13×10^8, so the gained results are TMTO divided by instruction per second in iPhone 5. Table 4.6 shows these results.

According to Table 4.6, the recommended mode of AES would be round 8 as ST that takes the attacker 1 h and 42 min to perform TMTO attack in this round and it is recommended for less than 2-h usage of mobile devices and also for higher time of mobile usage the recommended mode would be round 9 as LT that takes an attacker 447 years and 10 months to perform TMTO attack in this round and it is recommended for higher than 2-h mobile usage. The progressive difference in mathematical calculation of rounds 8, 9, and 10 makes the result of calculation so different. Table 4.7 introduces the suggested modes.

Table 4.7 AES-CCMP Proposed Modes

Mode 0	No Encryption	In Case the Data Is Not Confidential
Mode 1 (ST)	Round 8	Less than 2-h usage
Mode 2 (LT)	Round 9	More than 2-h usage

4.9 SUMMARY

The implementation of standard AES-CCMP is explained and the different parts of implementation are introduced. After reviewing problems of AES-CCMP in mobile devices, in this chapter a solution is provided. Three analyses based on 1-bit change of IC and 1-bit change of key in different rounds and interblocks and also attack analysis are done, supported with required data and graphs in which the reasons of properness and strength of the three proposed modes are analyzed.

CHAPTER 5

Conclusion

This chapter gives a general overview of the research and reviews the results of mentioned research. Also, the limitations in this project and recommendations for future research are presented.

Nowadays, different users are using wireless technology and a wide range of wireless devices such as PCs, laptops, tablets, and Fables can be found. Although this technology is being generally used, different devices have different capabilities in the usage. Since wireless networks have more vulnerabilities than other types of computer networks, preparing security in wireless local area network is essential. The security mechanism chosen for different devices may differ. A satisfactory security technique in wireless network is a balance between data security and network performance. The new mobile devices need security for the data transmission on the Internet, so the necessity of following security algorithms and protocols for encryption and decryption of the data becomes more and more important. For this purpose, the new devices have to follow the existing security protocols that are designed and implemented on nonmobile devices for Wi-Fi connections. IEEE 802.11-2012 encryption technique provides strong security mechanism in computer systems but it is not optimized in the usage of resources. Besides, in mobile devices that are power and resource constrained, the wireless connection speed decreases. The level of security provided in AES-CCMP is too strong for mobile devices since the mobility characteristic of mobile devices restricts the time required by an attacker to hack the victim device and the session would be terminated whenever the location of mobile device changes. So there is a lack of balance between security level and resource usage, which has been investigated in this study.

This study focuses on security models of the 802.11 standard that is named 802.11-2012. Emphasis of proposed technique is on confidentiality from CIA triangle and the focus of the study is on mobile devices.

Besides, this study proposes different modes of AES-CCMP for different durations of usage of mobile devices and investigates resource usage
in nonmobile devices.

5.1 PROJECT ACHIEVEMENTS

This section provides an overview of scope, objectives, purpose, and dec-
laration of problems that are defined in Chapter 1. Then, the results are
reviewed from the researches.

5.1.1 Overview of the Study

The aim of this research was to determine issues of the current encryption methods in 802.11-2012 used for mobile devices and to differentiate
modes of AES-CCMP for nonmobile and mobile devices for optimization of the technique and for speeding up network usage. The objectives
were to create two modes for AES-CCMP: one for portable systems that
have resource limitation such as tablets and phablets, and another for
systems that do not have resource and power limitation such as PCs and
laptops.

In addition, this research used C# language for implementation of
AES-CCMP and to compare different rounds of it changing 1 bit of IC
and 1 bit of key.

In addition, this research used C# language for implementation of
proposed method.

5.1.2 Review of the Results

The following conclusions can be drawn based on the findings of study:

1. Execution time: In mobile devices using AES-CCMP in rounds
   8 and 9 speeds up the execution time 20% than when using round
   10; for nonmobile devices, the execution time of classic AES-CCMP
   and AES-CCMP 256 is same and the proposed method has the same
   execution time as the classic method, although the security is strong
   when using AES-256.
2. Memory usage: Reducing two rounds of AES-CCMP, the memory
   usage would decrease 10–20% in comparison to round 10. The
   memory usage for nonmobile devices in AES-CCMP 256 does not

increase much compared with that in classic AES-CCMP (about 1%), which can be ignored. It can be claimed that two different algorithms use the same memory.

3. Security strength: In mobile devices AES-CCMP in rounds 8 and 9 is less secured than that in round 10 but the required security level is sufficient in relation to the kind of device and its specification of usage. Mobile devices have peer-to-peer connection, so it is most probable to disconnect a session during some hours, but in server–client topology of nonmobile devices the session is rare to disconnect. AES-CCMP 256 algorithm for nonmobile devices is resistant to all the known threats such as brute force, spoofing, replay, injection, etc. Besides, the method is resistant to precomputational attacks, a feature which is completely an opposite of classic method that is vulnerable to these kinds of attacks, especially TMTO attack, and that is why AES-CCMP 256 is recommended.

5.1.3 Implication of the Results

The results of this study indicate that using AES-CCMP in lower rounds for mobile devices makes them faster in network connection and satisfies the required security for them. In nonmobile devices AES-CCMP 256 can be optimized in resource usage using nine rounds but reducing one round is not efficient considering the costs of changing the protocol.

5.1.4 Limitation of the Study

In implementing this project, some limitations exist. The most important ones are lack of standard simulator for 802.11-2012 and limitation of hardware implementation of AES-CCMP.

As mentioned, lack of existing standard simulator for the mentioned method makes the whole project to implement and simulate from the base. Also, because of limitation of usage of OPNET simulator software, the simulation and implementation of proposed method in network environment is not possible. On the other hand, different mobile devices use different operators such as windows phone, Android mobile, IOS, Ubuntu, webOS, etc.; it was not possible to test the suggested method in all platforms, so it has been tested in only one platform that is windows based.

5.2 RECOMMENDATIONS

This section will present the recommendations based on both results and future research.

5.2.1 Recommendation Based on Results

It has been proved that nonmobile devices are going toward 256-bit key in AES-CCMP. It is recommended to test whether mobile devices can go toward 256-bit key in AES-CCMP as well. Mobile devices can also connect to nonmobile devices, so it is better to be homogeneous to be simple to connect.

5.2.2 Recommendation for Future Research

1. This method can be used in Multimedia Messaging Service (MMS).
2. This method can be tested in all mobile operating systems and nonmobile operating systems.

REFERENCES

[1] Amiri IS, Alavi SE, Idrus SM, Supa'at ASM, Ali J, Yupapin PP. W-band OFDM transmission for radio-over-fiber link using solitonic millimeter wave generated by MRR. IEEE J. Quantum Electron. 2014;50:622–8.

[2] Alavi SE, Amiri IS, Idrus SM, Supa'at ASM, Ali J, Yupapin PP. All optical OFDM generation for IEEE802.11a based on soliton carriers using microring resonators. IEEE Photonics J. 2014;6.

[3] Neo YS, Idrus SM, Rahmat MF, Alavi SE, Amiri' IS. Adaptive control for laser transmitter feedforward linearization system. IEEE Photonics J. 2014;6.

[4] Amiri IS, Alavi SE, Ali J. High capacity soliton transmission for indoor and outdoor communications using integrated ring resonators. Int. J. Commun. Syst. 2013.

[5] Amiri IS, Soltanmohammadi S, Shahidinejad A, Ali J. Optical quantum transmitter with finesse of 30 at 800-nm central wavelength using microring resonators. Opt. Quantum Electron. 2013;45:1095–105.

[6] Alavi SE, Amiri IS, Idrus SM, Supa'at ASM. Generation and wired/wireless transmission of IEEE802.16m signal using solitons generated by microring resonator. Opt. Quantum Electron. 2014.

[7] Sadegh Amiri I, Nikmaram M, Shahidinejad A, Ali J. Generation of potential wells used for quantum codes transmission via a TDMA network communication system. Secur. Commun. Netw. 2013;6:1301–9.

[8] Masica K, VRAP, LLNL, 2007. Securing WLANs using 802.11i. Draft. Recommended practices guide securing WLANs using 802.11i. Presented at the Control Systems Security Program (CSSP), United States.

[9] Osorio FC, Agu E, McKay K, 2005. Measuring energy-security tradeoffs in wireless networks. In: Performance, Computing, and Communications Conference, 2005. IPCCC 2005. 24th IEEE International, pp. 293–302.

[10] Habibi-lashkari A, Seyed-danesh MM, Samadi BV, 2009. A survey on wireless security protocols (WEP, WPA and WPA2/802.11i). Presented at the 2nd IEEE International Conference. Computer Science and Information Technology (ICCSIT), Beijing.

[11] McCarter HL. Analyzing Wireless LAN Security Overhead. Virginia Polytechnic Institute and State UniversityAU: Please provide the publisher location in Refs. [11, 13].; 2006.

[12] Ahmed Khan M, Cheema AR, Hasan A, 2008. Improved nonce construction scheme for AES CCMP to evade initial counter prediction. Presented at the Ninth ACIS International Conference on Software Engineering, Artificial Intelligence, Networking, and Parallel/Distributed Computing, Phuket.

[13] IEEE-Computer-Society, 2004. IEEE Standard for Information Technology – Telecommunications and Information-Exchange Between Systems – Local and Metropolitan Area Networks – Specific Requirements. Part 11 Wireless LAN Medium Access Control (MAC) and Physical Layer (PHY) Specifications. Amendment 6: Medium Access Control (MAC) Security, Enhancements. IEEE, p. 175.

[14] Ho Yung J, Joon Hyoung S, Jung Hee S, In Cheol H, Jun Rim C, 2004. Compatible design of CCMP and OCB AES cipher using separated encryptor and decryptor for IEEE 802.11I. Presented at the Circuits and Systems (ISCAS).

[15] Razvi Doomun M, Sunjiv Soyjaudah KM. Resource saving AES-CCMP design with hybrid counter mode block chaining – MAC. IJCSNS Int. J. Comput. Sci. Netw. Secur. 2008;8:13.

[16] Saberi I, Shojaie B, Salleh M, 2011. Enhanced key expansion for AES-256 by using even–odd method. In: 2011 International Conference on Research and Innovation in Information Systems (ICRIIS), pp. 1–5.

[17] Saberi I, Shojaie B, Salleh M, Niknafskermani M, 2011. Enhanced AES-CCMP key structure in IEEE 802.11i. In: 2011 International Conference on Computer Science and Network Technology (ICCSNT), pp. 625–629.

[18] Karri PMR, 2003. Analysis of energy consumed by secure session negotiation protocols in wireless networks. Presented at the International Workshop on Power and Timing Modeling, Optimization and Simulation, Torino, Italy.

[19] Keeratiwintakorn P, Krishnamurthy P, 2006. Energy efficient security services for limited wireless devices. In: 2006 1st International Symposium on Wireless Pervasive Computing, pp. 1–6.

Printed in the United States
By Bookmasters